GW00648012

Muhammad Ali

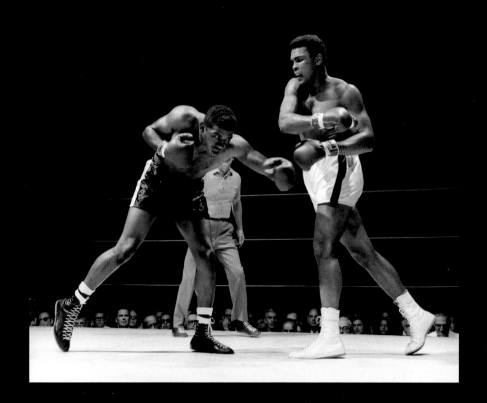

Muhammad A

Jane Benn

PULTENEY PRESS

Published by International Book Marketing Ltd
First published in 2009

Pulteney Press
1 Riverside Court
St Johns Road
Bath, BA2 6PD, UK

© Atlantic Publishing
For details of photographs copyrights see page 96

A catalogue record for this book is available from the British Library.
ISBN 978-1-906734-60-2

Printed in Indonesia

Above: Cassius Clay proudly receives his gold medal at the Rome Olympics in 1960 after defeating three-time European champion Zbigniew Pietrzykowski from Poland. Born in Louisville, Kentucky on January 17, 1942, Clay's boxing career was set in motion in 1954 when his bicycle was stolen from outside the Louisville Home Show at Columbia Auditorium. He had to report the theft to local policeman, Joe Martin, who was teaching boys to fight in the gym underneath the auditorium. Clay was intrigued, joined the gym and started learning to box. Six weeks later he won his first fight – and the rest is history!

Opposite: His younger brother, Rudolph, watches as Clay mixes pancakes in his home town of Louisville. When Clay returned home following his victory at the Olympic Games, he recited a poem – one of many such rhymes – making fun of his opponents and predicting the outcome of his fights.

Opposite: A smiling Clay arrives in London in May 1963, three weeks before his fight with Henry Cooper, the British heavyweight champion. Clay was keen to restore his reputation and re-assert his superiority with a decisive win. In his last fight against Doug Jones at Madison Square Garden, he had only just won on points in the final round.

Right: The handsome Clay was always well turned out and was proficient at self-promotion. When Customs officials at London's Heathrow Airport asked Clay the usual question, "Have you anything to declare?", Cassius Marcellus Clay launched into a monologue about himself – boasting of his boxing skills, his good looks and the outcome of the forthcoming fight in his typical flamboyant style.

Left: Clay leaves the Piccadilly Hotel in London and takes a walk with his promoter Jack Solomons, following his long flight from America. Despite the fact that he was already sharing a room with his brother Rudolph, the boxer asked for another bed to be moved in for his bodyguard as he announced that he was too precious to sleep on his own in a big city!

Opposite: His young sparring partner hooks a left to Clay's chin. Throughout his career the boxer always had a great deal of patience with children. He loved to entertain youngsters and was particularly adept at magic tricks!

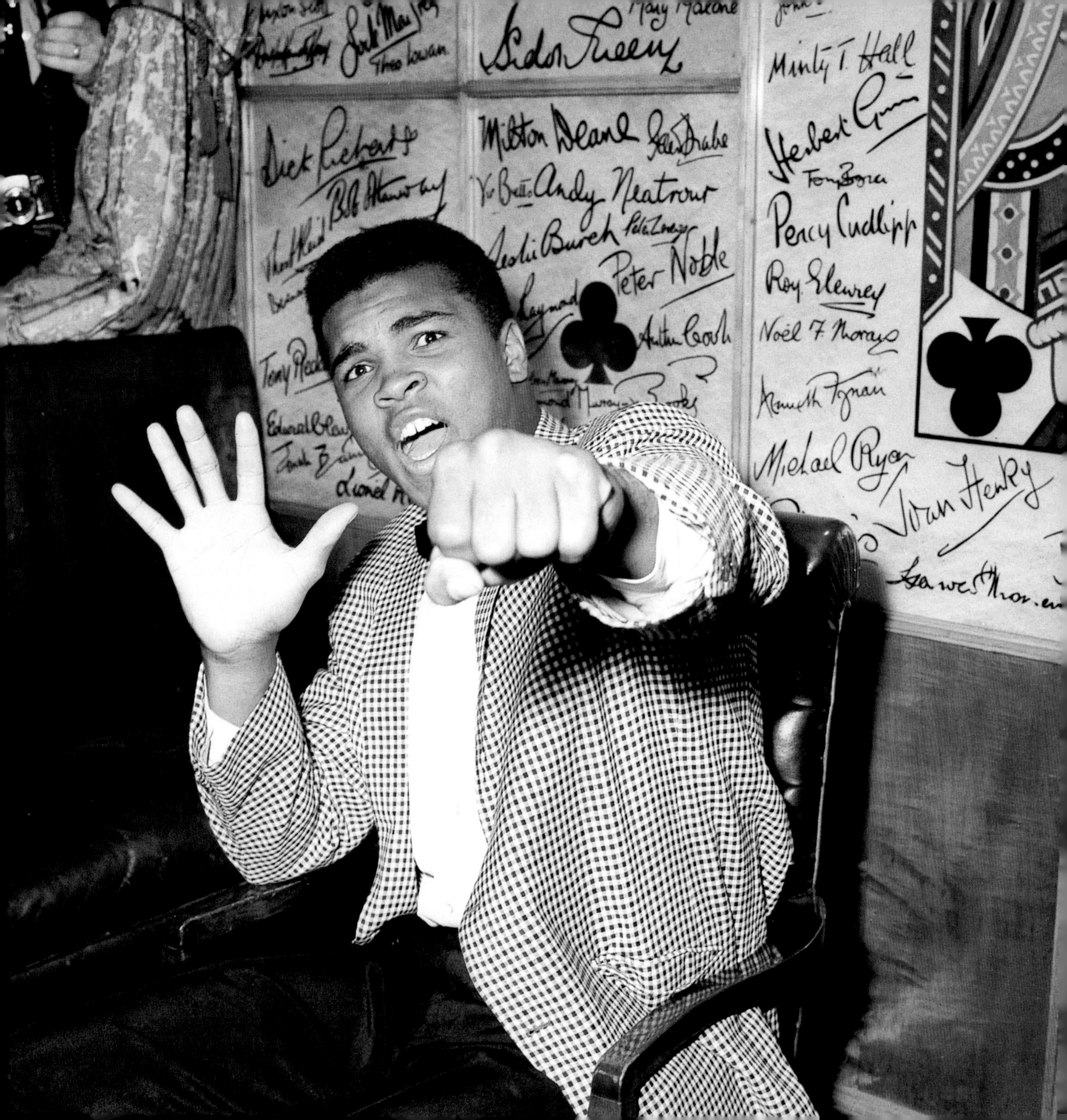
Peter Noble
Percy Cudlipp
Michael Ryan

Opposite: May 1963: One of Clay's favorite gambits was to predict the number of the round in which he would win his fight. Here he holds up his hand to indicate that he would knock out Henry Cooper in round five. He had originally predicted that the fight would only last three rounds, but amended it to five so that the 50,000 spectators would get their money's worth.

Above: The two fighters meet at a lunch arranged by Jack Solomons. Henry Cooper jokingly rolls up a napkin to ensure that he can hear what Clay has to say as the ever exuberant boxer continues to extol his own virtues!

Above: After a week of promotional visits, Clay finally begins his intensive work with his trainer Angelo Dundee at the Territorial Army drill hall in White City, London. After Dundee had laced his gloves, Clay trained with his sparring partner in front of a select invited audience.

Opposite: As media interest in Clay starts to grow, the charismatic boxer poses for photographers in the run-up to the fight with Cooper. This attention was reflected in the many articles written about Clay in the general press as well as in the sporting papers. Within a few months Columbia Records had released an LP appropriately named *The Greatest*, which included Clay reciting poems and soliloquies lauding his own talents.

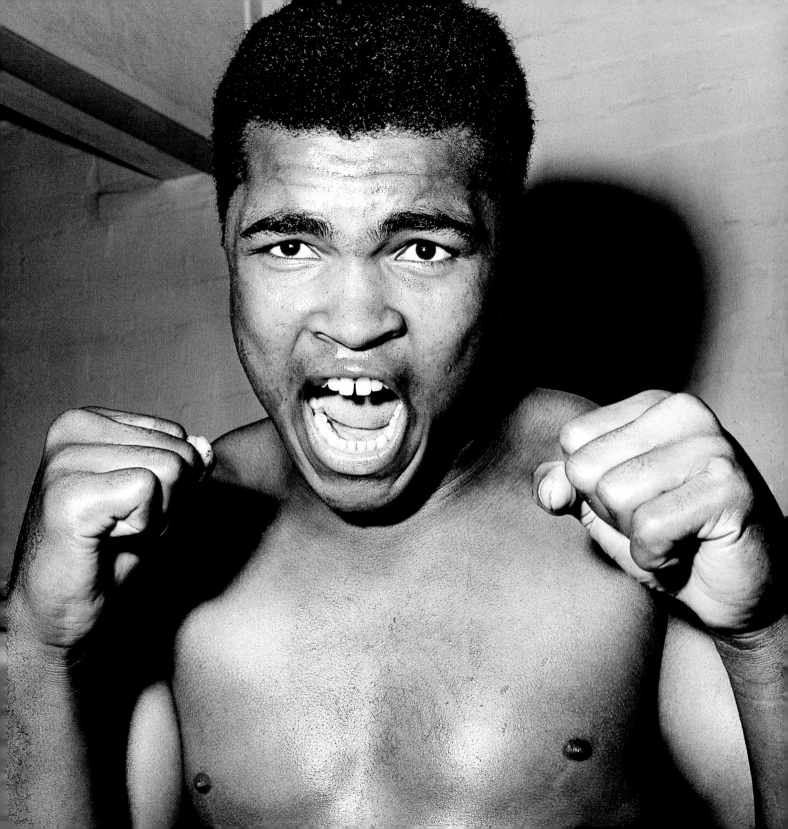

Opposite: Clay's younger brother, Rudolph, was also a boxer and trained with his older sibling in the ring as his sparring partner. The brothers belonged to a close-knit family and Rudolph became a long-standing member of the boxer's entourage – acting as his chauffeur and companion as well as a training partner.

Right: After rising early and limbering up in Hyde Park in London, Clay jogs down Lower Regent Street with another of his sparring partners, Jimmy Ellis. His training in the park included a series of fast sprints and was witnessed by a pack of journalists, who were most impressed with his level of fitness.

Opposite: Clay continues his training regime with a set of leg-strengthening exercises. His contact with the Louisville Sponsoring Group stipulated that he was to receive 50 percent of the earnings from his fights for the first four years. The remaining 50 percent went to his sponsoring group but included all the costs for management, training, travel and promotion and was considered to be a good deal for its time.

Right: Cassius Clay and Henry Cooper weigh in at the London Palladium at lunchtime on the day of the fight. Clay again holds up his hand to reinforce his claim that he will beat his opponent in the fifth round, while his smiling promoter and Cooper stand by. Clay weighed in at 207 pounds while Cooper was 21.5 pounds lighter at 185.5 pounds.

Above: At Wembley Stadium a crowd of 55,000 watched as Clay easily won the first three rounds of the fight and landed a barrage of blows that left Cooper torn and bleeding. Clay was also dominant for the majority of round four, but he was knocked onto the ropes by "Henry's Hammer" – Cooper's devastating left hook – at the end of the round. Clay managed to struggle to his feet and was saved by the bell. His torn glove was brought to the attention of the referee and Clay was able to recuperate while a replacement was found. He then came out and rained a series of blows in Cooper's face until the referee stopped the fight.

Opposite: Cooper's battle-scarred face meant that any direct blows could open up existing scars that bled easily. His fight injuries are evident for all to see as he poses with Clay after the fight.

Left: Following his victory against Cooper, Clay returned to his dressing room to find Sonny Liston's manager, Jack Nilon, waiting to tell him that he wanted to arrange a title fight. Clay immediately took every opportunity to brag that he would defeat Liston in round eight. He is seen here holding up eight fingers as he sits on his luggage while waiting for a car to pick him up from his hotel and take him to the airport.

Opposite: "I'm the greatest. Not only do I knock them out, I pick the round. I'm the boldest, the prettiest, the most superior, most scientific, most skilfullest fighter in the ring today. I've received more publicity than any other fighter in history. I talk to reporters till their fingers are sore," Clay boasted as he prepared to return to America.

Opposite: Clay relaxes during a training session for his forthcoming bout against Sonny Liston, the heavyweight champion of the world. The contract for the fight was signed in November 1963 even though most critics did not believe Clay could win against Liston's powerful punch. However, the contender had the utmost confidence in his own abilities, trained hard and studied Liston's technique.

Right: Clay poses during a training session in the Fifth Street Gym, Miami. He was always happy to put on a show for journalists, photographers and boxing fans. At this time rumors started to circulate regarding Clay's association with the Nation of Islam, sometimes known as the 'Black Muslims''. One of their most prominent members was Malcolm X, and Clay's association with him was regarded with much suspicion.

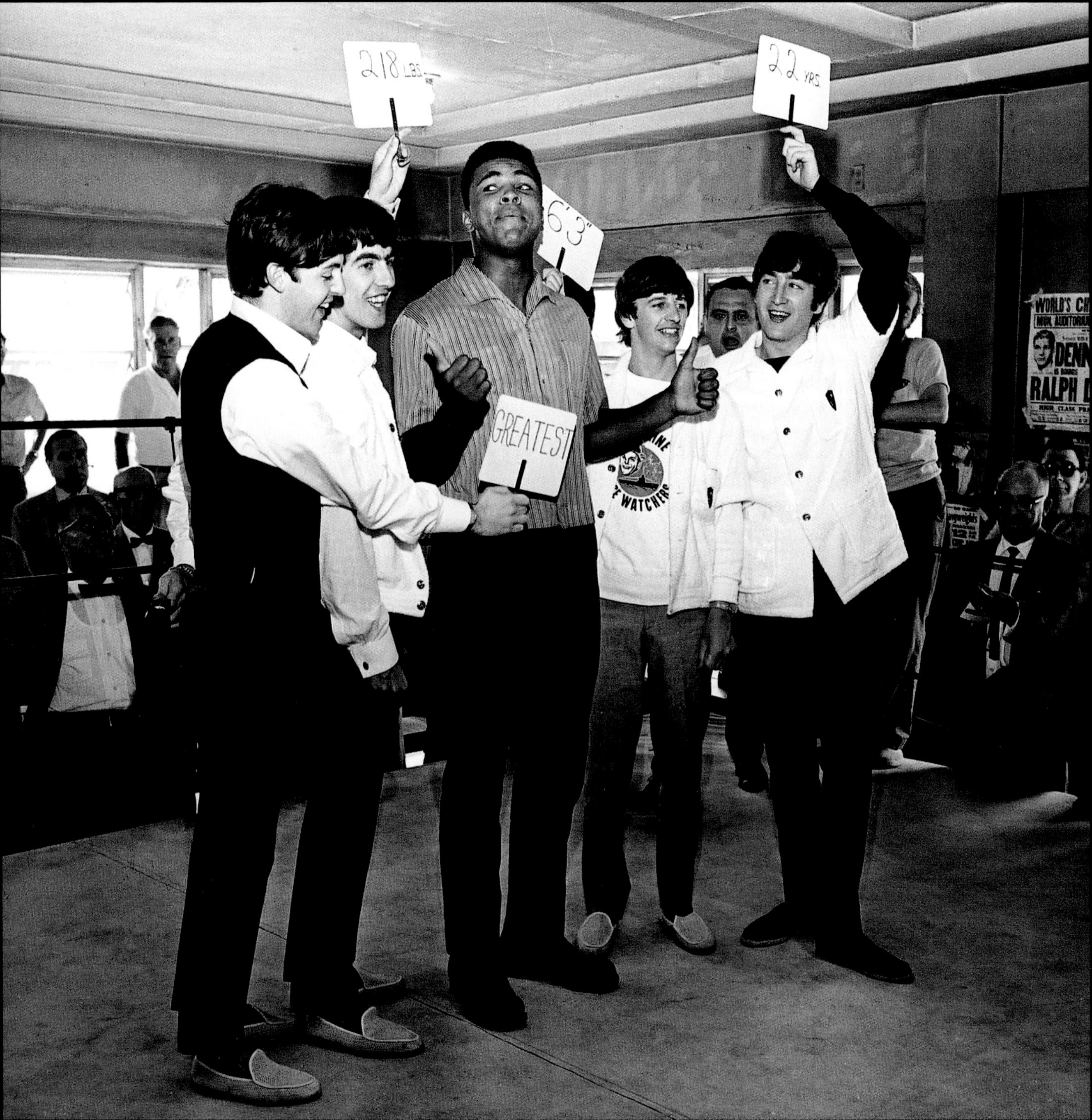
218 LBS.
22 YRS.
GREATEST

Opposite: At the same time as Clay was preparing for the big fight in Miami, the Beatles were in town for their second appearance on *The Ed Sullivan Show*. Clay was not a particular fan of the band but the publicity and photo opportunities were advantageous to both parties. Clay told the band that although he was the greatest, they were the prettiest!

Above: The championship fight against Liston begins at the Convention Hall, Miami Beach, on February 25, 1964. Clay danced around the ring and Liston was unable to catch him to land any of his legendary blows, which meant that by the third round Liston had begun to tire significantly. This gave Clay the chance to go on the attack and open up some cuts on his opponent's face.

Above: Clay spent rounds five and six ducking, diving and hitting Liston at will. Liston was unable to retaliate and at the beginning of round seven he quit in his corner because of a shoulder injury. Clay was the new heavyweight champion of the world, rushing around the ring proclaiming, "I am the greatest! I'm king of the world! I am the king!"

Opposite: After his title win Clay looks out over the arena, which was in fact half empty. This was due to a number of factors: many people did not believe Clay could win, ticket prices were high and rumors of his connection with the Nation of Islam had alienated many members of the public. However, as he left the ring he demanded that the gathered journalists acknowledge him as the greatest.

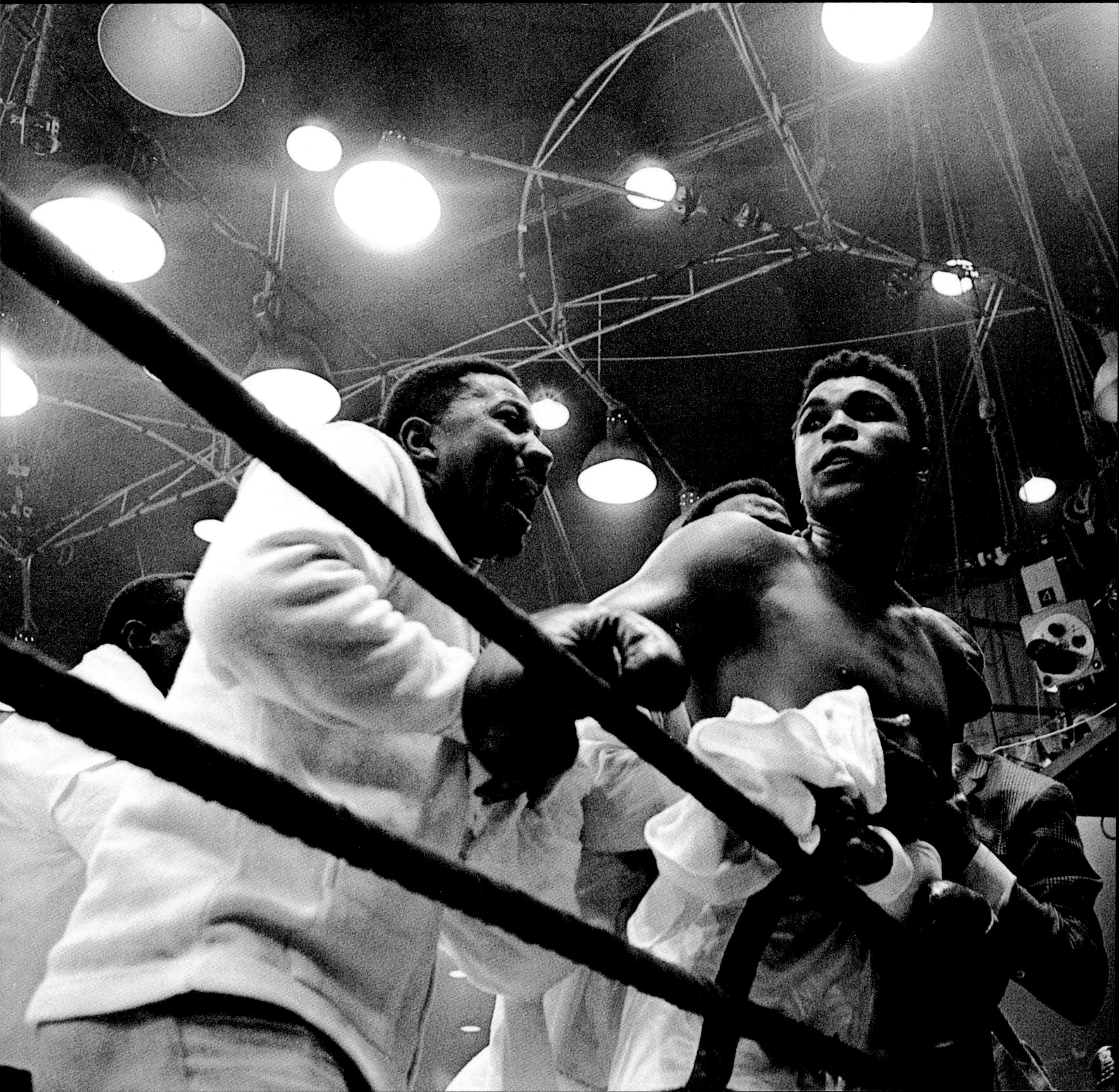

Above: Clay hugs his trainer Angelo Dundee. The two had first met in Louisville in 1957 but it wasn't until 1960 that Dundee began to work with Clay at the Fifth Street Gym in Miami.

Opposite: After the fight against Liston, Clay made it clear that he was a member of the Nation of Islam. The Nation was a highly unpopular organization that was seen as a potential threat to America. The views of the movement were very different from those of orthodox Muslims; they preached a radical message about the evils of white people.

Opposite: Shortly after his announcement about his membership of the Nation of Islam the champion renounced his "slave" name, Cassius Marcellus Clay, and confirmed that he wished to be known henceforth as Muhammad Ali, a name given to him by the leader of movement, Elijah Muhammad. However, the attitude of the American people was very hostile and the press refused to use his new name for quite some time.

Above: Ali prays at a mosque in Cairo on a trip to Egypt in June 1964. His conversion to Islam was still regarded with suspicion by the American public and it was deemed wise for him to leave the country for a few weeks. He spent a month visiting Ghana, Egypt and Nigeria before returning to America to prepare for a re-match with Liston.

Left: Ali's confidant and supporter Drew Brown, known as Bundini, wears a T-shirt with the slogan that became synonymous with Muhammad Ali, "Float like a butterfly, sting like a bee". It was allegedly invented by Bundini and was one of the many comments and jibes shouted out at the weigh-in for the first Liston fight.

Opposite: Ali continues to train for his re-match with Liston scheduled for November 16, 1964. Unfortunately Ali suffered a hernia three days before the fight and was rushed to hospital to have it repaired, prompting Liston to remark, "If he'd stop that hollering he wouldn't have a hernia." The fight was re-scheduled for May 25 the following year. This was more of a drawback for the older Liston, who had to work hard to retain his fitness, than for the younger, maturing Ali.

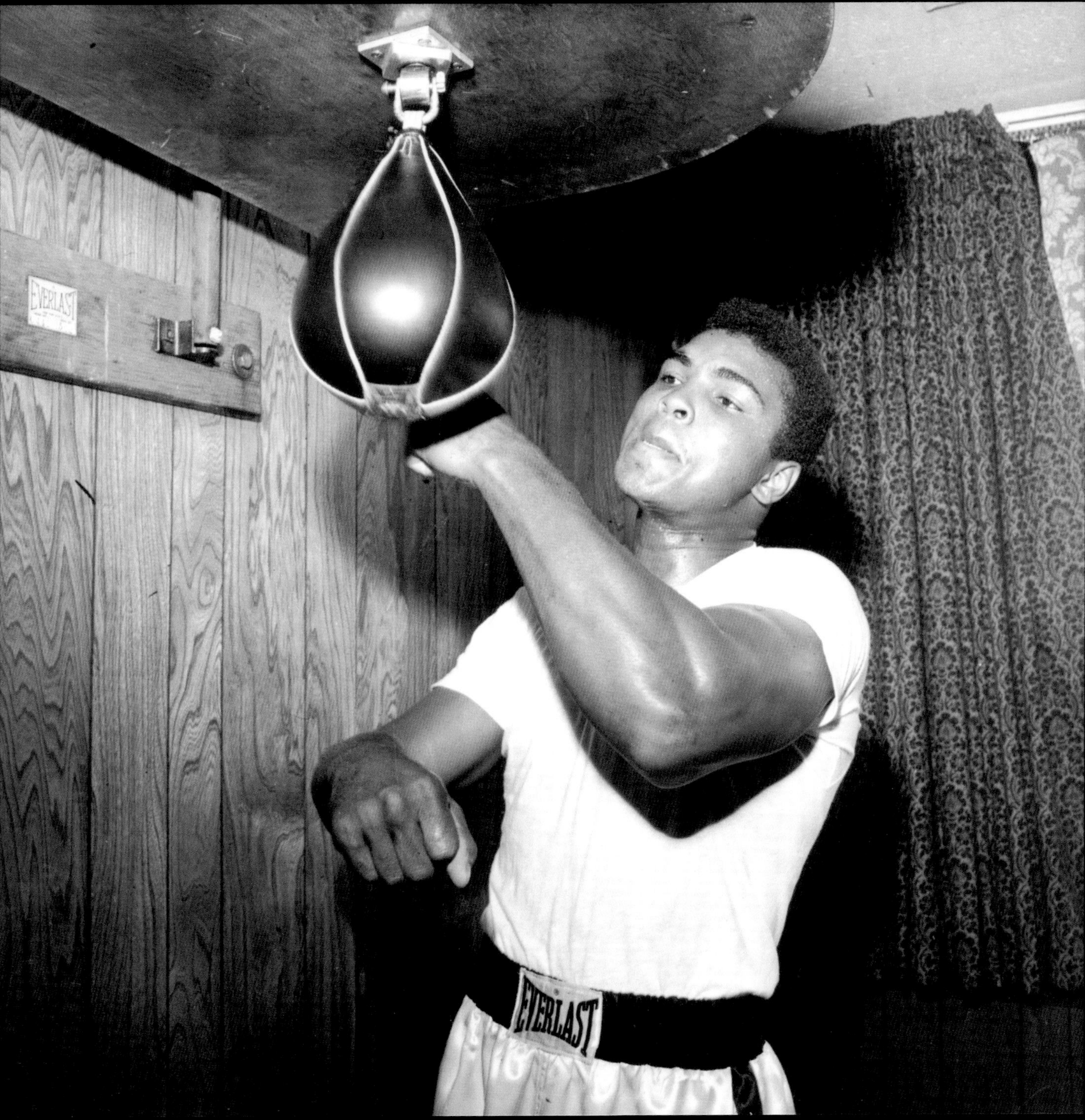
EVERLAST
EVERLAST

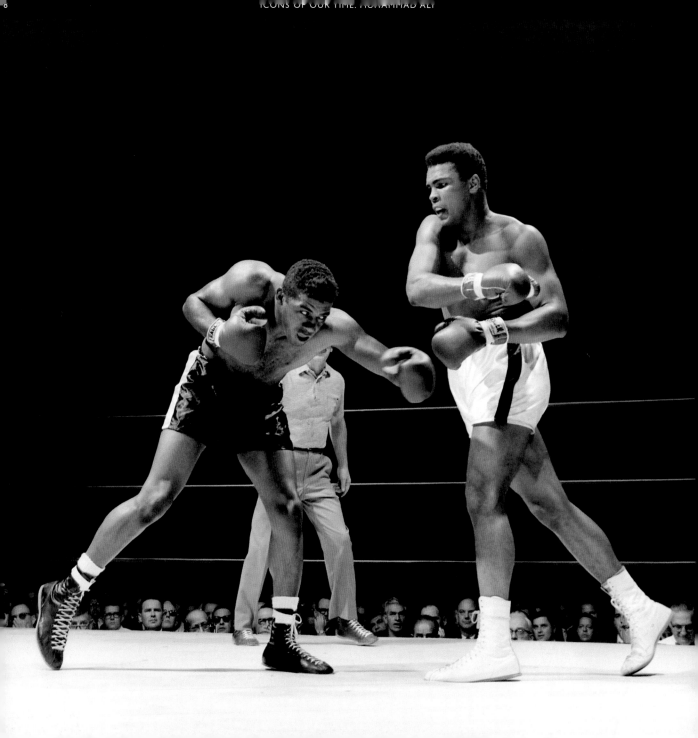

Opposite and above: Ali goes after Floyd Patterson in a world championship fight at the Convention Center, Las Vegas, on November 22, 1965. Patterson was completely outclassed and Ali toyed with him, hitting and backing off but not attempting a knockout, until referee Harry Krause stopped the bout in round 12. Following the fight he was heavily criticized for his tactics, but he defended himself by saying, "If I knock him out fast, you'd say it was fixed. If I knock him out slow, I'm a brute. I'm wrong if I do. I'm wrong if I don't."

Left: Ali was awarded the Edward J. Neil trophy as the Fighter of the Year 1965 at the annual awards dinner of the Boxing Writers' Association of New York – an honor that had first gone to Jack Dempsey in 1938. There was still a great deal of controversy surrounding Ali's abilities and his religious views. Former champion Joe Louis was one of many critics who believed Ali had been lucky in his victories and claimed that he couldn't punch or take punches.

Opposite: Ali gives a press conference as he arrives in London prior to his second fight with Henry Cooper. He had retained his world heavyweight title in March 1965 when he won in the 15th round after a long bout with George Chuvalo in Toronto, Canada. This was a difficult time for Ali as he had claimed exemption from the military draft, making his famous comment, "Man, I ain't got no quarrel with them Vietcong." Many Americans perceived him as a draft-dodger while Ali claimed to be a conscientious objector.

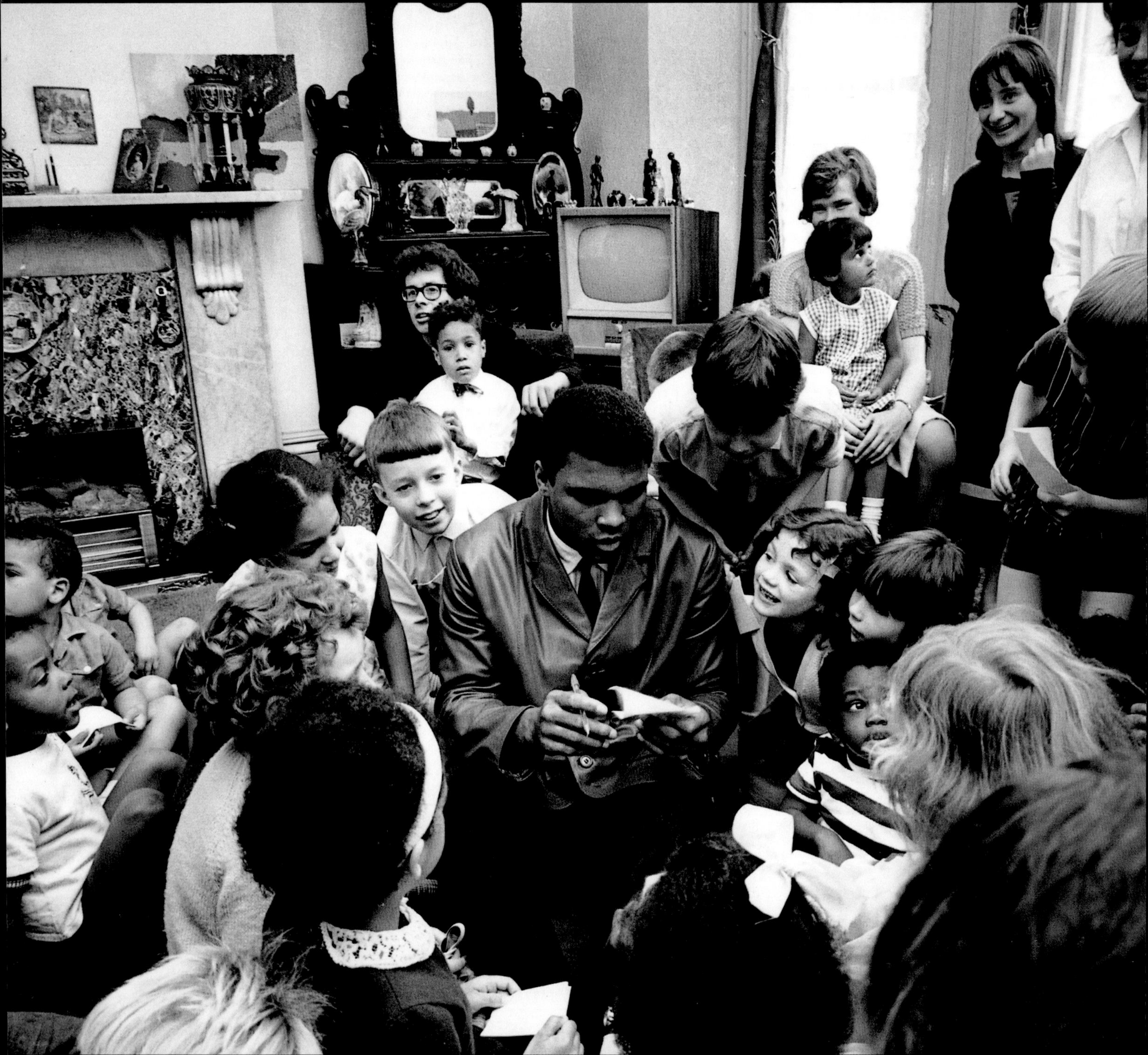

Opposite: Ali visits the London Free School in Tavistock Crescent, a social and educational establishment run by the residents of Notting Hill. He stayed for over half an hour, signing autographs and chatting to the children in an easy, relaxed manner. The visit had been arranged by Michael X – the British equivalent and friend of Malcolm X.

Above: As Ali leaves the London Free School, the passage to his car is lined with 24 members of the Racial Adjustment Action Society. This entourage had been organized by Michael X, who was concerned that Ali might be mobbed by local residents. On this second visit to London Ali was often met by crowds of cheering fans as he was now famous in his own right – not just in the world of boxing.

Opposite: Ali has tea with his trainer, Angelo Dundee, and his manager, Herbert Muhammad, in his London hotel. Although most heavyweight title bouts had historically been fought in America, it was becoming increasingly difficult to arrange fights on home territory owing to Ali's unpopularity with the American public. A title fight was therefore arranged in London with Henry Cooper, the British heavyweight champion – the biggest fight that had ever been staged in England.

Above: Promoter Harry Levene watches as Ali and Cooper compare their reaches at a press conference before the title contest. During the pre-fight build up Ali was uncharacteristically subdued and refused to give any predictions for the fight, explaining that he no longer felt he had to prove himself as he was the reigning heavyweight champion.

Opposite: Ali walks along Wardour Street in London after a morning press conference. He firmly believed that Allah would protect him from harm, so did not feel the need to take excessive security precautions and enjoyed mixing freely with his fans.

Right: An immaculately dressed Ali holds up the award given to him by the Boxing Writers' Club. He was a stylish dresser and clothes invariably hung well on his six foot three inch perfectly proportioned frame. He had an unmistakable interest in fashion and one of his trips out in London had been to Cecil Gee, the men's outfitter in Piccadilly.

Above: While training at the Territorial Army Gym in White City, London, Ali stops to have a chat with some of his fans.

Opposite: Ali trains with his own 83-pound punch bag, which had been flown in specially from America. As was often the case, he was watched by a large crowd of fans and admirers keen to see The Champ in action.

Opposite: Ali's trainer Angelo Dundee tapes his hands ready for a sparring session at the Territorial Army Gym. Ali's sparring partner was an old friend from Louisville, Jimmy Ellis. They had been training together since Dundee had brought Ellis to Miami before the first Cooper contest in 1963.

Above: The title fight against Cooper is just over a week away. There was a strong belief in Britain that Cooper could win the world title, particularly as he had almost knocked Ali out in their previous encounter. However, at 32 Cooper was more than six years older than Ali and he continued to suffer from thin, weak tissue around his eyes that cut easily.

Left: Ali pounds and pummels his
personal punch bag. It had cost a great
deal of money in excess baggage to fly
this important piece of equipment in
from the United States.

Opposite: Angelo Dundee fixes Ali's head
protector before a sparring session. At
this time one of the core beliefs of the
Nation of Islam was that all white
people were devils. This view was
obviously not embraced by Ali himself as
both Dundee and his personal physician,
Freddie Pacheco, were white – and Ali
got on well with them both. Indeed
Dundee remained Ali's trainer and
mentor throughout his boxing career.

Above: Ali always has time for his fans, no matter how young they are! Eight-month-old Maria Morin seems singularly unimpressed by the great man.

Opposite: Ali lands a hefty punch on Jimmy Ellis during one of their sparring sessions. He often let Ellis hit him quite hard – regarding it as effective preparation for competitive contests, helping to sharpen his reflexes and build up stamina. The last training session for both Ali and Cooper took place on May 19, 1966 – two days before the title fight.

Left: Twelve hours before the contest Ali weighs in at 201.5 pounds, his lightest ever fighting weight. Cooper was 13.5 pounds lighter at 188 pounds, 2.5 pounds heavier than when Ali beat him in June 1963. Huge crowds were outside the Odeon Leicester Square and more than a thousand people witnessed the weigh-in.

Opposite: Cooper swings a left hook as the title contest begins at Highbury Stadium – home to Arsenal Football Club – on May 21, 1966. Over 45,000 spectators were there to watch, as well as more than 200 members of the press. Every single seat was sold although there were a number of two-guinea standing-room tickets remaining. A further 30,000 paid to watch on television in Britain and a massive audience of over 20 million were able to watch in America, thanks to satellite technology.

Left: Cooper throws a punch at the start of the bout. This stunning left hook was his main weapon, although he had been practicing throwing punches with his right in training sessions. Ali's speed and agility in the ring meant that few of Cooper's blows landed on their target as The Champ danced around the ring.

Opposite: Ali throws a long right towards Cooper's bleeding face. Ali opened the cuts above Cooper's right eye at the beginning of the sixth round after the challenger had taken a battering from a series of left hooks earlier in the fight. Referee George Smith stopped the fight 1 minute 38 seconds into the sixth round because of the damage to Cooper's eye. The cut later required 12 stitches.

Opposite: A pensive Ali looks out from the top of the Post Office Tower in London as he prepares for his title fight against Britain's No. 2 heavyweight fighter, Brian London, in August 1966. A contest with Karl Mildenburger due to take place in Germany in September was also very much in his thoughts as he pronounced, "I've got two fights on my mind and no heavyweight of the world should have that."

Left: Ali was keen to rebut suggestions that he was not taking the forthcoming championship fight against Brian London seriously enough. He had been maintaining his usual thorough training schedule since he arrived in London.

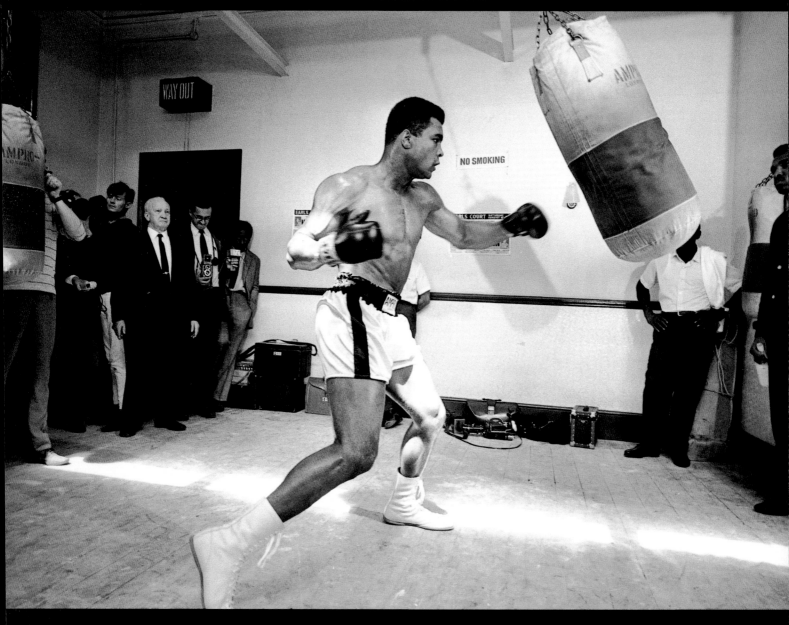

Above: The defending champion attacks the punch bag with vigor and aggression for a full five rounds to demonstrate his stamina and level of fitness. Ali also went seven rounds with his sparring partner Cody Jones who had been chosen for his similarity in weight and build to Brian London.

Opposite: Ali works out in the ring at The Noble Art Gym in London's Havistock Hill. He having problems maintaining his motivation as he was not convinced that Brian London was a worthy opponent.

Left: Training for the fight against Brian London continues in a sparring session with old friend Jimmy Ellis. Ali's swift reactions help him avoid a straight left from his sparring partner. During these sessions Ali had a visit from Henry Cooper. Their feelings of mutual respect were evident as the pair shook hands. Ali had visited Cooper in his dressing room following the fight three months earlier to apologize for the way the fight ended. Cooper responded by saying, "It was a pity. We were really enjoying ourselves. But I would have done the same to you if I could!"

Opposite: Ali weighs in before the title fight at Earls Court on August 6, 1966. London weighed in at 200.5 pounds – 9 pounds lighter than Ali's fighting weight of 209.5 pounds. Ali was 8 pounds heavier than when he fought Cooper in May 1966.

Opposite: Promoter Jack Solomons watches as Ali shakes hands with Brian London at the weigh-in.

Right: London ducks away from one of Ali's punches. However, he was totally out-classed by the lightning reflexes and speed of the champion. The bout ended in the third round when Ali knocked London to the ground with a killer right. The contest was relayed live to American TV. It could only be seen on CCTV in theaters in Britain, although it was broadcast live on BBC radio.

Left: Ali knocks out Zora Folley in the seventh round at Madison Square Garden in March 1967. Since taking the world heavyweight title from Sonny Liston in 1964, Ali had successfully defended it nine times.

Opposite: Ali spars with local children outside his home in Miami. He had been called to report for military service, despite the fact that he was claiming conscientious-objector status. Ali's refusal to comply with the demands of the Armed Forces resulted in a conviction for "refusing to be inducted". In April 1967 his boxing license was suspended and his passport taken away – thus effectively ending his boxing career for the foreseeable future.

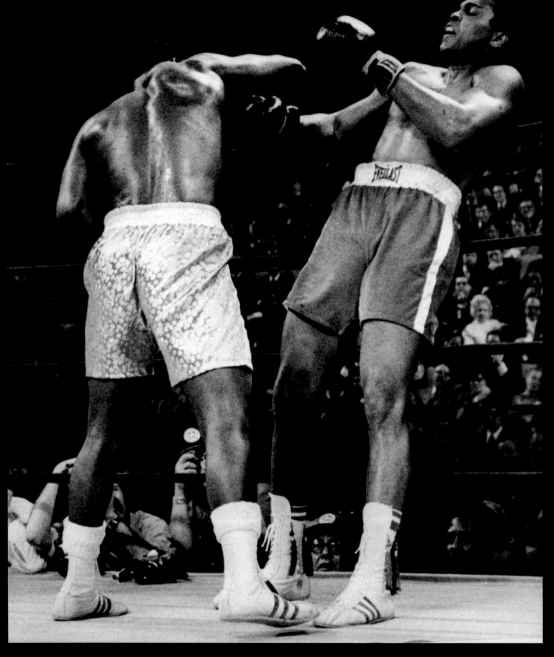

Left: Dubbed the "Fight of the Century", Ali's comeback fight at Madison Square Garden on March 8, 1971 was watched by 20,000 spectators. After his boxing license had been restored in 1970 this title fight was soon arranged with Joe Frazier and for the first time two undefeated heavyweight boxing champions were to go head to head. However, it was soon apparent that after three years without competitive bouts Ali was not as quick and fit as he used to be. Although Ali managed to survive to the end of the 15th round, referee Arthur Mercante awarded the fight to Frazier. Both boxers were bruised and battered, and a philosophical Ali remarked, "Just lost on points, that's all..."

Opposite: Unlike many boxers, Ali's good looks were never permanently affected by being punched.

Above: Ali meets his old adversary Henry Cooper in London for the first time since their championship fight in May 1966. Ali and Cooper shared some banter and Cooper invited his former opponent to join him in his new hobby – playing a round of golf!

Opposite: British and Empire heavyweight champion Jack Bodell meets guest of honor Ali at a dinner given by the World Sporting Club in London on October 18, 1971. Following his defeat by Frazier in March 1971, Ali spent a couple of years traveling the world fighting exhibition matches.

Opposite: Ali attends a question and answer session at the London School of Economics arranged by the institution's Islamic Society. In the years following his exile from professional boxing Ali had found a way to earn a living by appearing on the college lecture circuit. His lectures were based on topics that were close to his heart and he was known to spend many hours perfecting his speeches.

Right: Ali jogs along with his twin daughters, Rasheeda and Jamillah – managing to combine his training with family life. Ali had married his second wife, Belinda Boyd, in 1967, after his divorce from Sonji, whom he had married in August 1964. Although Ali was devoted to Belinda he had a reputation as something of a womanizer.

Opposite: While Ali was traveling round the globe participating in exhibition bouts, his goal was always a re-match with Joe Frazier in order to win back the world championship. He was hugely disappointed when George Foreman beat Frazier early in 1973 to take this title. His next scheduled fight was against Joe Bugner – a contest he was expected to win easily.

Left: Ali sits thoughtfully before the Bugner fight at the Convention Center in Las Vegas, Nevada, on February 14, 1973. In one of his training sessions he had made the mistake of goading his sparring partner Tony Doyle – who then smacked Ali in the face three times in succession and stopped him dead in his tracks.

Left: Ali vs Bugner: There were few
exciting moments in the contest
and, as predicted, Ali had no
problems dodging Bugner's jabs and
punches. Ali had entered the ring
wearing a flashy robe emblazoned
with "People's Champion" – a gift
from Elvis Presley, one of Ali's
heroes.

Opposite: Ali dodges yet another of
Bugner's blows as he wins his tenth
professional fight since being
defeated by Frazier in 1971. The
manner of Ali's easy victory led
many to believe that it was time for
him to have another crack at
winning the world title.

Above: Ali plays with a lion cub in Jakarta, Indonesia, as he prepares to take on Rudi Lubbers in October 1973. His previous two fights against Ken Norton earlier in the year had emphasized the need for proper training and preparation. He had only trained for three weeks before his first match – and lost in the 12th after Norton broke his jaw in one of the earlier rounds. This experience had a significant impact on Ali, and although the re-match again lasted 12 rounds Ali was victorious in the end.

Opposite: A contemplative Ali was convinced that he was ready for the challenge against his former opponent. When asked why he did not throw many right punches against Lubbers in his last fight, Ali quipped, "I'm saving it for Joe Frazier."

Opposite: Despite his three-year break, Ali looks in good physical shape as he eagerly anticipates his rematch against Frazier arranged for January 1974. Public interest in the fight was high, especially after both boxers became involved in a brawl when they appeared on a television show the evening before the bout.

Above: Ali and Frazier at Madison Square Garden in 1974. Ali won their second contest in the 12th round. The more mature Ali was proud of the fact that he could take any punishment meted out to him now that he was not as fleet of foot as he once was.

Opposite: Ali chops wood at his training camp in Deer Lake, Pennsylvania. It had always been his dream to possess his own facility. He operated an open house policy, welcoming visitors of all ages, but was particularly fond of spending time with children there. Ali loved to visit the camp with its log cabins, beautiful views and clear air, and trained here throughout his fighting career.

Right: Ali knocks out reigning heavyweight champion George Foreman at the famous "Rumble in the Jungle" in Kinshasa, Zaire, on October 30, 1974. Throughout the fight Ali adopted his "rope-a dope" technique where he would retire to the ropes to rest, letting his opponent punch away and tire himself out. In the eighth round he abandoned this tactic and let rip with a straight right to Foreman's chin, knocking him out and once more becoming champion of the world.

Opposite: Joe Bugner squares up to Ali outside the Dominion in Tottenham Court Road, London. Ali had come to London to watch Bugner, the European heavyweight champ, fight American Boone Kirkman at the Royal Albert Hall on December 3, 1974. Bugner was very keen to have a go at the world champion and a fight was arranged for later in 1975.

Above: Kirkman had to withdraw from the impending Bugner fight because of a broken nose and was hurriedly substituted by Argentinean Alberto Lovell. However, he was no match for Bugner and the bout was stopped in the second round. The ever ebullient Ali stripped off his shirt and the two pugilists entertained the crowds by staging a mock fight through the ropes.

Left: Ali looks surprised as he reads the headlines in the London *Evening Standard*. He was to announce that he was 99 percent certain he would retire after the upcoming bout with Joe Bugner scheduled for June 1975 in Kuala Lumpar, Malaysia. Ali dominated this fight and won on points, as expected, in the 15th round.

Opposite: Ali hugs actress Annazette Chase, who played his second wife, Belinda Boyd, in the film *The Greatest*, which was made by Columbia Pictures in 1976 and released in the following year. The film was a highly fictionalized account of Ali's life and starred the charismatic boxer and many of his entourage. Simultaneously Granada Publishing released Ali's biography, *The Greatest*, co-written with Richard Durham, editor of the newspaper *Muhammad Speaks*. Ali spent a few days in Britain giving press conferences and signing copies of this best seller.

Opposite: Ali sits next to his daughter Hana at a lunchtime press conference to promote his biopic, *The Greatest*, at the Café Royal in London. Ali married Hana's mother Veronica Porche in June 1977, ten months after the baby was born.

Above: Time to relax with his third wife, Veronica, who was never very far from Ali's side as he traveled all over the world. Although they owned a beautiful mansion in Los Angeles, they spent very little time there.

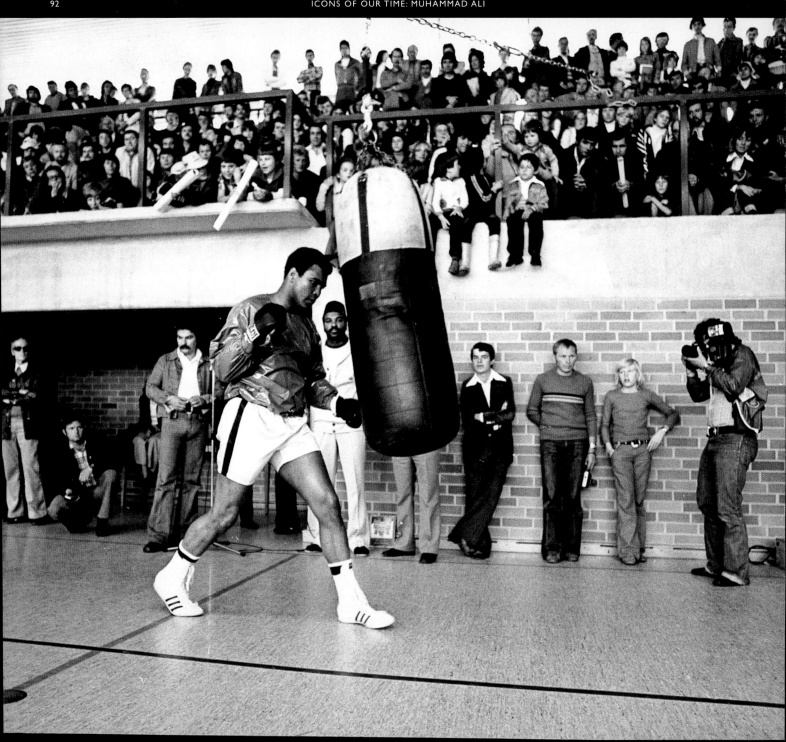

Opposite: Ali works out in a gym in Munich as he prepares for his title fight against England's Richard Dunn in 1976. He had successfully defended his title against Joe Frazier in the infamous "Thriller in Manila" in October 1975 when the fight was stopped in the 14th round. This was followed by an easy victory against Belgian Jean-Pierre Coopman in Puerto Rico and a much less convincing win against Jimmy Cooper. In the latter bout Ali weighed in at 230 pounds – the heaviest in his boxing career – which had a detrimental effect on his speed and agility.

Above: Dunn steps forward with his right foot to try to land some hard right jabs in front of The Champ. Ali responded by raising the pace and flooring his adversary with blows from with his fearsome right. Dunn kept getting up and coming back for more punishment but the fight ended when the referee finally counted him out on his feet in the fifth round.

Right: Ali arrives in London with his daughter Hana for a two-day visit in 1978. In 1978 he fought Leon Spinks twice, losing and then regaining the world heavyweight title. Ali held the title until 1980 when he was defeated by Larry Holmes in Las Vegas. Two years later, he fought for the last time, losing to Trevor Berbick in the 10th round.

Opposite: Ali chats with fans in 1983. When he finally retired from boxing he had fought 61 professional fights, only losing five of these, and had won the world heavyweight title three times. His charisma and flamboyant personality, together with his formidable boxing talent, contributed to his massive popularity and to the award of Sports Personality of the Century at the BBC's final sporting awards ceremony of the millennium. To quote George Foreman, Ali was "a great champion who transcended the sport of boxing".

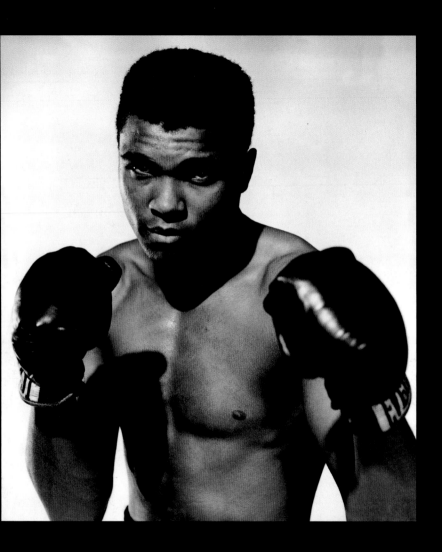